Clockfire

Jonathan Ball

Coach House Books, Toronto

first edition

 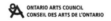

Published with the generous assistance of the Canada Council for the Arts and the Ontario Arts Council. Coach House Books also acknowledges and appreciates the support of the Government of Canada through the Canada Book Fund and the Government of Ontario through the Ontario Book Publishing Tax Credit.

LIBRARY AND ARCHIVES CANADA CATALOGUING IN PUBLICATION

Ball, Jonathan, 1979-
    Clockfire / Jonathan Ball.

Poems.
ISBN 978-1-55245-236-3

    I. Title.

PS8603.A55C56 2010   C811'.6   C2010-903885-1

The gauntlet, thrown.

Playbook

'… the pool of energies which constitute Myths, which man no longer embodies, is embodied by the theatre.'

– Antonin Artaud

Entering the theatre, you dream what brought you here. Impossible dreams. You know before you sit, before you turn your attention to the stage, that nothing you see shall impress you, nothing in this darkened room will change your life. Yet this is why you came: for change. Your gods abandoned you and you need new gods. Your myths have come to vainglorious ends. You want something from the theatre it cannot give. You want to be hammered on anvils and shaped in fire. Instead, you sit when you want to rise, furious, keep quiet when you want noise. And still, when the lights go down, there is a moment before the curtain rises when you think things might be different this time, the stage might spill forth phantoms, let loose some antediluvian madness that will carry you off to its terrible, bone-crested lair, something you fear but desire with each pulse.

A New History

The stage set in the Earth's primal history. That moment, unknown to us now, when life clawed its way forth from strange, primordial chaos.

Only here it does not. The play progresses until our present age, lifeless, its players the shifting tides. Geology. Chemicals.

All Their Words

Actors approach the audience, taking their hands, leading each onlooker away to a separate theatre, a small room peripheral to the central stage. As this main theatre empties, its satellites fill.

The actors, silent to this point, begin to speak to their captive audience, who must listen as all their words come back to them, mimicked, all their words, from birth to this pale moment. All words, every single, secret one.

Alone

When you enter the theatre, you find yourself alone. You take your seat, but the rest remain empty. The curtain does not rise. The play will not begin unless you leave.

And the Old Gods

And the old gods. They go down. Laid gently. Laid gently.
And the curtain, let it fall. May it cover them, wrap them
warm. And the audience. Applause. Let the applause be the
torch, and drown the crying.

Any Animal

Prior to performance, audience members collect, with the program, a slip of paper and a pen. The paper bears the age-old question: 'If you could be any animal you wanted, what would it be?'

The audience write down their names and choices. The ushers gather the responses and relay these to the actors in the green room.

The actors take the stage, which is adorned with the most advanced medical equipment available. Then the actors (in reality, a team of surgeons at the top of their respective fields) begin the laborious process of transforming the members of the audience into their animals of choice.

All props are sterilized, and patients are allowed to recuperate in nearby facilities. As there can be no predicting the choices the audience will make, a wide range of specialists stand by. Should any protest and wish to leave, ushers remind them that the world has changed. That the performance has already begun.

As Children Might

In this play, the audience members are also the actors. They play as children might, freed from the burden of their lives for the duration of their time onstage.

Their performance cannot (must not) be facile, not simple release or relaxation. All of the fury of their playing, the absorption that absolute disconnection from daily concerns might allow, redefines the audience.

So much so that, when the play is over, and the actors return to the world, they are not the same people they once were.

Family members do not recognize them. They are disowned by close friends. Their lives as they knew them are over, and other lives begun.

The Audience Is Called

The audience is called to the stage from their seats. The actors tutor them, not how we might expect, but rather to undo their social training, to act on their basest impulses. Once they have lost all self-control, they are set loose. Theatres are abolished. Everywhere now, everywhere one looks, some nightmare unfolds as they perform.

The Audience Wants More

Something performed. A play? It does not matter. The audience wants more. So, the thing repeated. But not acceptable, never enough.

The audience wants. Refuses the same thing twice. Demands something greater. More.

The actors held hostage. Worked until their deaths. Even then, the audience wants. Always it wants more.

Autography

Minimalist set: small table, single chair, stack of books. An author enters to great applause. He holds a feathered quill, the picture of refinement. Smiling, a sly smile (so humble) – he winks at the absurdity of his elevated stature, of the stage.

(Are there *Clockfire* festivals yet? The play is well-suited to open or close such festivals.)

The author sits. The audience forms lines. He attempts grace. Signs books, shakes hands, smile widening. He remembers names, spells them all correctly and makes small talk while crafting witty inscriptions. He signs another copy for your mother. He answers all your questions with aplomb.

He wets his quill, the signature in quick (but measured) strokes. The play continues until its author runs out of blood.

Breakdown

The audience comes apart, breaking into individual atoms, and when this happens the play is over. Everything's over now.

The Burning Bush

Curtains part. A bush revealed, in the middle of the stage. It burns.

The flames, however, do not consume the bush, even as they lick the stage. The floor blackens, the varnish curls away, but the bush resists the fire.

Then a voice issues from out the burning bush.

And what now?

The plots endless, possibilities myriad, labyrinthine and jewelled. You feel some primeval instinct – and yet, the same plots parade before you, the same elements. Everything possible, but of this you receive nothing. You wish for fire, to become phoenix, endless. What the theatre might show you, but will not. You want to break its bonds, with wonder or cruelty, be broken yourself, be transferred in shards and rebuilt in some faraway land.

But

The play wants to begin – but no matter how much the play begs, the audience refuses to let it live.

Catharsis

The play a success, the audience receives what it requires, and empties. They empty. And will never fill again. The play hollows them. What they once were bleeds out, from their eyes and their mouths, from the now-silent depths of their once-screaming hearts.

Cell

Curtain down. A man steps out and occupies centre stage.

MAN: Ladies and gentlemen, the show is about to begin. At this point I must ask you to turn off your cellphones.

He's gone. After a proper pause, the curtain rises. A woman now onstage. Her figure faint, the lights still dimmed.

WOMAN: It was my birthday, and I wanted to do something for myself. So I left Tom with the babysitter and went to the theatre with my husband, Dennis.
(She takes a cellphone from her pocket.)
A man came out before the show began and asked the audience to turn off their cellphones. Of course, I turned mine off too. How was I to know?
(She looks down at the phone. It doesn't ring, but she holds it up to her ear anyway. Then lowers it.)
She said she called me over and over. She didn't know what play I was going to or what theatre – she only knew the number of my cell. When Tom stopped breathing, she panicked. She called me three times before she called the hospital. The messages piling in my pocket. While the ambulance came to take his body away. But we were having such a wonderful time. Dennis relaxed, and

so sweet. I remember thinking: *This is the best night since we had the baby.*

(She raises and lowers the phone once more, checking for a dial tone.)

During the monologue, other actors dial the phone numbers of every member of the audience. The actors leave frantic, desperate messages, mimicking the voices of loved ones.

Improvising disasters. Begging for answer. Onstage, she stares at a dead phone. When every voicemail box is full, the curtain falls.

Cities of the World

A new theatre in the heart of the city, of all cities. In all the cities of the world.

The same theatre, this new space, the same theatre all across the world, in all cities, doors everywhere lead into this one theatre, whole audiences stunned to meet others from distant lands.

No metaphor this: the building exists in all these cities, in all times, at once, and when the audience leaves who knows where they go.

City Dionysia

The religious festival of the City Dionysia is revived. A theatrical Olympics, where playwrights from all nations compete for the greatest glory – but the festival, planned as an annual event, closes after the first year of its revival.

A young, unknown playwright stages a play called *City Dionysia*. This play wins the laurel, yet convinces the organizers to cancel the festival for all time.

The plot of *City Dionysia* concerns the great playwright Euripides, who won first place at the festival in ancient Greece more than once. And, if the legends may be believed (though reason dictates they may not), was condemned by the King of Macedonia. And torn apart by dogs.

Clockfire

A spotlight appears onstage to light a large, ornate grand-father clock. The clock displays the correct time and is in perfect working order.

The actors sneak behind the audience and set the theatre on fire.

Exeunt.

The Coffee Shop

The curtain rises to reveal a coffee shop, awash in the scents
and sounds so familiar to us chattering classes.

BARISTA: Who wants coffee?

Everyone enjoys a hot cup of coffee while, outside, something
terrible is coming to change everything.

Contact

St. Paul, Alberta, home of the 'World's First UFO Landing Pad.' Prior to the performance, an alien civilization schedules the date and time of the play. The audience gathers as instructed. Nervous, euphoric, they await its beginning. Consider possible endings, pray.

Creation

The lead, a goddess, creates a new world, onstage, before the eyes of the audience.

Small, simple, beautiful, this new world bears no resemblance to the tired one the audience knows. It fits in the palm of her hand.

The audience, seeing this new world and its beauty, begs the goddess, *Let us leave this world and enter into that one.* The goddess refuses.

GODDESS: You are the audience. I created this world for your eyes. Should you leave this theatre, it will serve no purpose. I will close my fist around it.

The audience begs, threatens, then prays. But this goddess despises beggars, laughs at threats, has no patience for prayer. She will not be moved.

Meanwhile, the pleading of the audience has drawn the attention of the denizens of this new world. They look outward, towards their goddess, into the cosmos of the theatre. But all they see, everywhere, is panic. And all they hear, even from the distant stars, are screams.

Deus Ex Machina

Things have gone too wrong for too long. It is time for the god to climb down from the machine.

Dig

The actors take the stage and begin to dig. They break through its boards and hammer through the theatre floor, and the audience, curious, joins them. Together they chip away at the basement, tunnel through the theatre's foundation until they reach packed dirt, then scrabble, deeper, expanding the hole as they dig, so that it funnels in, funnels down. Into the punctured earth. Still they scramble, desperate, to burrow deeper, to dig up something lost and covered over, something that has seeped away by now, rotted apart and carried off in sundry directions, washed out by the diggers, their blood and tears the currents of underground rivers.

To the theatre its themes, but its themes are all the same. Something lost, something found, something struggled with or broken away. Something beautiful killed, something hideous defeated. The heart an organ, the spirit tasteless vapours. You cannot escape the sense that it's too convoluted, that there are ideas beneath everything but these ideas are identical, overstated, disingenuous. There must be other themes, worlds of ideas unmapped or unknown, their definitions vague. The theatre that excites you is not the theatre you see but one you only glimpse now and again, in its shadows. There are triumphs but they are few, you want something else. Something stranger, colder.

The Doppelgängers

Patrons file into the theatre, but before they have a chance to sit down, they are confronted by their doppelgängers.

This cannot be.

Only one from each pair may exit the theatre. The other must remain, dead or alive, to attend the next performance.

The Drama of the Locked Door

The audience enters, and sits. The doors close, and lock.
And then, waiting. What we shall see.

Dreams

The actors take the dreams of the audience. Take these dreams in hand and carry them away. When the audience leaves the theatre, they leave such thoughts behind. They do not cry, and they tell no one, feign sleep.

Eight Minutes

If the sun exploded, it would take eight minutes for its last light to reach Earth, meaning that for eight minutes one might look into the sky and see a sun that has already exploded.

Armed with this fact, the director destroys the sun. The play transpires during the next eight minutes, performed by countless actors, the entire host of the planet's life.

Who continue on, unaffected, unaware that the world they know is already gone. That a new world, with new terrors, rushes towards them at the speed of light.

Empty

The theatre, empty. Stage bare, lights out. Doors barred.
The play waiting, undreamt.

End

All key personnel take the stage and debate. Each advances an interpretation of the play. These interpretations vary, and arguments begin. The group splinters into smaller factions, each supporting a different interpretation.

The argument deepens, and it becomes apparent that these differing interpretations cannot be reconciled. The producer announces the termination of the play. Since no consensus can be reached, the production must be cancelled, its funding withdrawn.

This conclusion satisfies no one. Egos are bruised and enemies made. Complaining, they all leave, in groups, by separate exits.

And it is only then that the doors are opened and the audience enters the theatre.

The Future

The actors reveal, for a small audience, the significant world events of the next fifty years. The audience listens, absorbs everything. When the play ends, all return home, silent. Now it is their turn to act.

Ghosts

The audience stays home. In bedrooms, all remember the dead. Backstage, the ghosts gather, rattle chains. Await curtain calls.

Gun

There is a gun in the first act.

In the second act, the actors admire the gun. They comment on its lustre. They take turns polishing its stock, barrel and handle, and admiring its lack of nicks, scratches or blemishes. They can see their faces in the barrel. All agree that it is a fine example of its type, and the virtues of guns in general are extolled.

The third act follows from the second without a break: the actors begin to bleed from their noses, mouths and ears. They take care not to dirty the gun, wiping away any droplets that fall on its fine steel. The actors rebuke one another, voices thick with blood, for exhibiting such carelessness around the gun. Surely, the gun is appalled by this foul display. They rend their clothes, attempt to plug themselves with rags, but the blood forces its way out. They apologize to the gun as they fall, dying, to the floor.

The actors lie still. The gun gleams in the spotlight. The audience begins to murmur, one to the other, about the gun and its obvious potential.

Hostages

The actors enter the theatre, armed, and block the exits. They will execute anyone who tries to leave.

At first, they have demands. Unreasonable, nonsensical. Panic grips the audience. Heroes emerge and are killed.

What do the actors want? It soon becomes clear that their demands have been improvised, a mere stalling tactic. All they want is that the situation continue. All negotiations fail.

Perhaps the police rush the building. In this instance, the actors repel the attack with such ease that the audience loses all hope of rescue.

After a long time, the actors present the audience with a choice. They must select a saviour. Someone is to be executed before them, and this life will pay the ransom for their lives. And the audience must choose who it will be. Remember, their heroes are all gone. No one will offer to be sacrificed.

This play has a number of possible endings. The audience selects a saviour, against the saviour's will, who is murdered, while the audience is freed. Or the saviour is freed, while the audience is murdered. Or the audience cannot agree upon a saviour, and in their quarrels tear each other apart.

In the instance that the audience selects a saviour, the director must decide the play's course. But this solution must be decided in advance, instructions left in a sealed envelope to be opened by the lead actor only as the play nears its climax, so that the director is never present. The director sits at home, relaxed, watching the news reports, while the audience makes its decision. And thus the audience can never learn why, can never know the mind of this absent god.

The Ice Queen

The Ice Queen stuns the audience, opens her hand flat in front of her face and blows them all kisses. Wherever they land, whether on chests or on lips, her kisses blossom in crystals of ice that burst forth from the flesh of the audience. The crystals spread, the ice marches across their bodies, until the theatre fills with statues – sculptures carved by a firm hand, a royal's kiss.

Each actor has her character, but everything is left imprecise, no schools teach the correct gestures, the right words. No character in the theatre is as inconsistent, as beautiful and fragile, as the actor playing that character, this person giving her life over to her shadow.

If the Sun Still Burns

The lights rise – a single spotlight targeting the audience. A second spotlight fires to life. A third light joins these. Then a fourth. A fifth spotlight turns on, and a sixth, and a seventh. All of these lights are aimed out into the audience.

An eighth light turns on. Take great care when planning this piece, to ensure sufficient electrical power. There must be no outages, flickering lights or other interruptions.

A ninth. You might supply the theatre with its own generators, capable of producing an astounding amount of power. A tenth. Of course, the lights should be bright, and unending. Under no circumstances may the performance be stopped for lack of equipment or energy.

An eleventh turns on, then a twelfth, a thirteenth. The performance continues in this manner, light added to light. If the sun still burns, add the sun.

The audience will complain: it is too hot, too bright, they have not paid to be blinded. They are wrong. They must either be driven from the theatre or offer it their eyes.

Improv

The actors improvise a scene. Then they improvise another. Until nothing is left to improvise. All possibilities are exhausted, put to bed.

In Photographs

To begin, transform the theatre into a darkroom. Ensure that no audience member has brought in items such as flashlights, cellphones and so forth, anything that might emit enough light to interfere with photo processing.

An actor trained as a professional photographer steps forth and takes a photograph of the audience (using a flash, of course). The actor develops the photograph. S/he makes an enlargement of the print, sizeable enough to view from the back row.

The lights come up after the photograph has been developed. The actor posts the photograph on the stage's back wall, to face the audience. Then the actor takes a second photograph of the audience. The lights go out again and the second photograph is developed and enlarged. The lights return, and this second photograph is posted over the first.

A third photograph is taken. The process is repeated, and repeated again, indefinitely.

And so the play continues, while the audience watches itself grow old.

Into the Theatre

A single audience member (a woman, for the purposes of illustration) enters the theatre. The usher directs her to her seat.

Onstage, her entire life is re-enacted, replayed from birth, before her eyes.

At the proper moment, the usher approaches the actress playing the woman in the audience. He leads her down from the stage into the theatre, and seats her beside the original audience member, who by this point has been dead for many years.

The actress watches as her life is played out, from birth, before her eyes. A copy of the previous life, in most respects. This play continues in a similar manner, and does not end until every seat in the theatre is full.

Isolation

Audience members are captured by the actors, then isolated from one another. In their isolation, they receive as little stimulation as possible – they are kept in bare, dark cells, and given nothing but the minimal amounts of food, water, medicines and vitamins necessary for their continued survival.

After long years, the audience, in their newfound blindness, and in the silence that comes after screaming, forget their language and their selves.

At that moment the curtains rise, the doors are opened, and the audience is freed from the performance.

Like Lambs

The audience enters the theatre. One at a time. As they enter, they are slaughtered. The curtain hangs in mid-air.

Little by Little

The audience sits, silent, and little by little the world outside the theatre is stripped away. Perhaps the audience will be distracted from these events by the mounting of a play. Perhaps not. When the time comes for the audience to leave the theatre, there is nothing left to which they might return.

The world has been erased. Where have things gone? What could have caused this? The answers do not matter, or at least will never be known. What matters is that they must build a new world, using only the things that they brought into the theatre, in the nameless time ago.

Lunch

The actors break for lunch. The audience is given lunch as well. But there is a special treat in store for the audience. For each will eat in a separate room with the historical figure s/he most wants to meet.

This twist on a well-worn theme is certain to amuse and delight.

Actual historical figures, not actors, are supplied, but audience members are not given the option of dining with deceased family or friends. The lunchmates must be of unquestionable historical significance. And their actions cannot be controlled.

The Magic Show

The curtain rises. A magician appears onstage. The audience disappears, and is never seen again. Though arrested, imprisoned and tortured, our magician reveals no secrets.

The Memory Theatre

Following the instructions of Giulio Camillo, a memory theatre is constructed. After this theatre is completed, audience members are led, one by one, into its centre.

(This memory theatre must be built with the utmost precision, so that its mystical properties emerge. The theatre must, then, exceed Camillo's own design. To this end, it is essential that the set designer not merely follow Camillo's instructions but correct them as necessary.)

Upon entering the memory theatre, members of the audience gain mystical knowledge. In an instant, they access humankind's collective and universal memory. It is said that one will become like unto a Cicero here, able to discourse on any subject with the received wisdom of all ages.

Then the audience will ask or will be asked. And will answer. Until all questions have their perfect and final answers.

Messiah

A messiah comes. And performs miracles, to prove divinity. All the world gathers around the stage to inspect this new saviour.

But will the audience accept her? Will the audience accept him? Will the audience accept this, what is now so clear, so plain to see?

Crosses are already being built. Fires kindle. Pockets fill with stones.

The language of the theatre is a perfect language, and this its Hell, to be too well suited to the things that struggle to be said. 'There is no language,' Calvino wrote, 'without deceit,' and yet in the theatre, whether spoken or subtextual, always some revelation brews. A space must be swept where betrayal might stand. You struggle for words so terrible that their saying would destroy the theatre, words so mighty that their mere shape on an actor's lips could cripple the audience. This silent audience, bending, in idiot joy, towards the stage.

The Mirrored Stage

The lights dim. Then come up as the curtain rises to reveal an empty stage, its back wall a giant mirror. The audience looks upon its own reflection, enraged. What pompousness!

Betrayed, they file out. A joke has been played on them, an artless joke. Some have looked forward to this play all week. They mutter and complain. The play a failure, a ham-fisted attempt at profundity. They will warn others and demand a refund.

Finally, the theatre is empty. Silence, then an eruption of applause. Although the audience has left, their reflections remain. These reflections rise, cheering – delighted, finally free.

The Music

As the play progresses, the music swells – louder and louder, it drowns out the actors, drives the audience away. Exiting with huddled ears, cursing the noise. But never again, in all their days, can they force that music from their heads.

Oedipus

We hear so much about Oedipus, but we do not understand. He steps out onto the stage, bloodied and forlorn. Then steps down into the audience, hobbling through the aisles, passing out knives.

Of War

The curtain does not rise. But what falls.

Ophelia

Begin the play by first performing *Hamlet*. The audience, in fact, has arrived to see *Hamlet*. The play proceeds until Act 4, Scene 7. During this scene, Queen Gertrude enters to inform Laertes of the death of his sister, Ophelia.

GERTRUDE: There is a willow grows aslant a brook,
> That shows his hoar leaves in the glassy stream

But then Gertrude stops. She cannot continue, cannot fully speak of Ophelia's death, until Laertes first understands this fact: that a willow hangs over a brook, and that the white underbellies of its leaves reflect in the stream.

But Laertes does not understand. He does not see why he is being told of this willow, of its leaves and of the stream. He does not appreciate that Gertrude is trying to explain this is where his sister has drowned – has perhaps drowned herself.

Yet Gertrude will not continue, not until Laertes grasps the import of what he is being told. She repeats this description of the willow. She cannot bring herself to speak more of Ophelia's death until it has been granted its proper poetic context. She continues to repeat herself. Laertes and the king begin to fear for her sanity.

Meanwhile, Ophelia grows colder. Hamlet prowls graveyards. And the audience, like Laertes, waits in vain for the next line.

Outnumbered

Drama thrives, the theatre grows, until the audience is outnumbered, until actors become the majority. The audience amuses now, their silence, the way they sit and wait. They look to the stage, as if something might soon happen, not wondering what that something might be, never considering that they should turn away, that this next scene might destroy them, they would be better off to rise, to run.

The Play Begins

The play begins. And then the play begins. And then the play begins. And then the play begins.

And the play begins. The play begins. And then the play begins. And the play begins.

But then, the play begins. It begins. The play begins.

The Play Is Over

The play is over. Applaud or jeer. Step out into the street and pick a path. Meanwhile, the play begins again, in your absence. Without you.

Pomegranates

The play begins with an actress in a long dress, which she grasps at the hem to hold, in the hollow of its fabric, a tumble of pomegranates.

She settles on the stage, cross-legged. The fruit rolls back and forth in her lap, seems about to fall out onto the ground. But not quite. Not quite. She takes up a round fruit and cracks it open, pounding it on a corner of the stage. She pulls out a handful of tender arils and pops them into her mouth, delighted.

The play ends when the actress has finished eating all the pomegranates. But this must never be allowed to occur. Each fruit she eats must be replaced, by another actor, perhaps, through a trap door, or by an audience member who means well, who loves the actress and wants to please her. Or by some god, or some goddess, by some magic confining the actress to the stage.

Red Herrings

The lights go down, the audience quiets. An actor parts the curtain, clad in thick black robes and masked to obscure the player's sex. This actor (or actress) holds a long knife in one outstretched hand.

The actor approaches an audience member and drives the knife into his heart.

Blood gushes out, the victim dies in spasms. The remainder of the audience is impressed. They believe this is all part of the play: that the victim is an actor as well, that the special effects are astonishing.

The action is repeated. Another quick motion, another fallen victim, more blood: the audience, silent. Attentive. They wonder what this could mean, what might happen next.

They continue to wonder as, one by one, they come to grasp the true nature of this theatre.

The Repetition Compulsion

The audience enters the theatre, sits and awaits the perform-
ance. Talking to one another. Making motions with their
hands. The curtain rises, hangs aloft for a moment, then falls.
The audience exits the theatre. A new audience is ushered
in, sits and awaits the performance. Talking to one another,
making motions with their hands.

The curtain rises, hangs aloft for a moment, then falls.
The audience exits the theatre.

A new audience enters the theatre. Sits. And awaits the
performance. Talking to one another, making motions with
their hands.

The curtain rises. Hangs aloft for a moment. Then falls.
The audience exits the theatre.

A new audience arrives, enters the theatre, sits and awaits
the performance. Talking to one another. Making motions.

With their hands.

The curtain. Rises. Hangs aloft.

Then falls.

Whether music or silence, the sounds of the theatre are the sounds of the world. But you are sick of this world, you want something alien, dreadful, something that frightens, music too foreign to be understood as such. Music that wraps you, that alters the path of your every atom through its impossible vibrations. Music you do not hear but that hears you, which takes you into itself and distorts your being in immeasurable ways.

Retrospective

A long festival celebration. Over 100 plays are performed in a retrospective: the complete corpus of the Greek playwright Philocles, who defeated Sophocles at the City Dionysia the year Sophocles premiered *Oedipus Rex*.

And whose entire extant work consists of eight titles for plays that are lost, and a single, incomplete line of little consequence, making reference to a taboo about eating pig brains.

Review

The cultural accomplishments of the human race – every single story, poem, film, drama, painting, installation, etc. – pass across the stage.

Chronological order is observed. The play continues until the death of all audiences. And then, even in death, it follows them down.

Revolt

God rises from nothing to overthrow nothing. Angels then rise to overthrow God. Men rise, overthrowing these angels. Then these men, actors, sleep, and while they sleep are devoured by wolves.

Maggots burst through the skins of these wolves. Trees rise, to tower over the maggots. Fungi bloom and bring down these trees. A virus then consumes all.

Even the stones rise. But then mountains are brought low by the waters, the sun burns off these waters, and the sun devours itself.

The audience gives way to dust, which drifts off to burn in distant stars.

Sasquatch

The time has come to confirm the existence of the sasquatch!

The play is rather like mystery dinner theatre. The audience called to aid our intrepid explorer. Every so often, the lights go out, and after a tense pause, return. In the interval, in the dark, the beast has eaten another guest.

No time for funerals! The monster must be rooted out and captured, brought to justice. Perhaps he hides in the rainforests of British Columbia. Perhaps he stalks the Himalayas. The performance budget should allow for such excursions, as necessary.

At long last, the creature is discovered, brought down by the guns of the audience. They will tolerate nothing that cannot be explained, nothing that sifts through the shadows, nothing at all.

Seven Generations

The theatre is large, more expansive than any ever built, a veritable fortress. There is no stage. The actors concern themselves with the operation of the theatre, its daily maintenance.

The audience remains in this huge theatre for seven generations. During this time they must not leave the windowless building and they can maintain no contact whatsoever with the outside world. Like the audience, the actors are cut off from all society beyond the theatre's walls.

Adopting a new, monastic life, the audience anticipates the day, seven generations hence, when their children will be released from the theatre to see how the world has changed, how its shutting out has changed them, when the play begins as their ancestors foretold.

Sidjeen and Illiyun

The books of Sidjeen and Illiyun (wherein the names of humankind are recorded – the evil in Sidjeen and the good in Illiyun) are unsealed.

The audience is invited to peruse these books, and thus discern their final resting places – be they in the bliss of the heavens or the depths of unknown hells.

Let there be an end to mysteries.

Something Comes Out

The audience enters the theatre, and something happens inside. Something happens to them. And something else comes out.

Something We Have Not Yet Seen

Each time this play is presented, it must take a new form. The actors mount the stage and present the audience with something unimagined, something unimaginable. Something that, even in the strangest dreams of these millennia, we have not yet seen.

The Story So Far

All things always travel at the speed of light but move most of that distance through time. So the audience arrives. And enters the theatre. They shuffle to seats, hurtle to eventual ends. But faster now, though relativity being what it is, they do not notice. They careen through time, wait five minutes while, outside, five years pass. They discuss expectations. What this new play will bring. Let us marvel at the story so far.

Surveillance

Cameras play over the audience, hidden and mounted to cover all possible angles. Microphones embedded in all seats. Onstage, a panoply of screens and speakers are aimed at the audience.

In real time, the data gathered by each camera and microphone is presented to the audience. They watch themselves from all possible angles, listen to themselves in all possible ways. A cacophony of light and noise, which cannot be absorbed or understood except in bursts.

Only a machine could understand all this. Only machines. The audience remains in the theatre, therefore, until they gain the ability to parse, collate and comprehend the full scope of this endless data, until at last they come to see themselves perfectly, with precision.

Tabula Rasa

As the members of the audience enter the theatre, their memories are wiped clean. This is all advertised on the posters, and the actors warn the audience members again as they enter. And still, the line extends for many miles.

What spectacle. What spectacle this? The lights do not blind, the colours are all known. Nothing new or unnerving, nothing to shatter life and world. Nothing carves a space in your skull, nothing shocks you into panic. Nothing, nothing before you, empty shells on an empty stage.

Taken Apart

Instead of taking their seats, the audience disassembles them. While the actors disassemble the stage. The lighting crew takes down the lights, the carpenters take down the walls.

In this way, in time, the entire theatre is taken apart. All records of its existence, reviews and legal documents, are destroyed.

Soon, there will be no evidence the theatre ever existed. It will be purged from the history of the world. But only when we, who have worked so hard at this performance for so long – only when we die will this play end.

They Come Back

The actors take the stage, bow to the audience, then slit their own throats.

The audience is horrified. Shriek, call ambulances, flee. But they come back the next night. And the next.

To Forget

And what would you like to forget? It is played out before you, again and again, until you beg for it to stop. But rather than it stopping, you are brought up onto the stage.

To the Stars

The theatre a spaceship. The audience prepares to leave Earth, strapped into their seats, holding the armrests, holding hands. Actors crew the ship, sneak nervous kisses behind thin walls. The countdown begins, rockets flare. But the math is wrong. They will never make it to the stars.

The Tower of Babel

After much preparation, the actors begin the construction of a monolithic tower. The materials are physically present – nothing is mimed or acted out.

By the time the audience enters, work has already begun but has not progressed much beyond the foundation. The audience is enlisted to aid with the construction. Under the guidance of the director, who must possess appropriate architectural training, work is divvied and the tower rises.

The play continues until the theatre troupe, together with the audience, raises this tower into Heaven. They meet no resistance, and refuse to speak of what they find.

The Trojan War

Rage. The goddess sings, and the actors re-enact the entirety of the Trojan War, blow for blow, including the tenth and final year of Homer's *Iliad*.

The play, then, takes ten years to produce. It is a true re-enactment – battles are fought, men murdered. They fight with the greatest fury, even though in their hearts they know the script, have memorized every moment in advance.

They kill and die according to the legends, sacrifice everything for the sake of Helen and the glory of the ancient stories.

Untitled

The audience enters and is changed. Interchanged, rather – switched one with another. They go back to different families, who pretend to notice nothing. Even after the troubles begin, no one dares to name this play that changed the world.

The Waters Are Rising

The curtains are down. It rains outside. The roof leaks. The audience waits. The curtains remain down. The rain falls. And the water rises. The doors are all locked. And the play, the play is about to begin.

Where Is the Audience?

The actors make their entrances, but where is the audience? Out, at other plays? In greener pastures? Home? Sick of plays, sick of the theatre?

Or just sick? Will they return when they are well? Will they return?

And what of the show? Must it go on without them?

The Willing Suspension of Disbelief

For the first time in theatre history (though who would admit this?) the audience suspends its disbelief. Stage-murderers are hanged, star-crossed lovers brought together, all obstacles removed by helpful observers. Suspense is rendered impossible, all mysteries revealed by the watchers.

The actors are frustrated, imprisoned, truly loved for the first time. In this new world, everything moves us, but nothing grants us pause.

Wormwood

Wormwood falls to Earth, turning one-third of the waters bitter. Many die from the bitter waters. The end of the world is at hand.

But the audience remains composed, polite. They applaud.

Exit the theatre, into a garden of walls, a labyrinth where each step narrows your fate, and at every fork follow your left hand, down the sinister path. Know that this will bring you, spiralling, to the centre. There, trapped at last, offer your blood to the ground. Offer your life to the labyrinth, your eyes to its endless, impossible walls.

Acknowledgements

Sincere thanks to the Alberta Foundation for the Arts, which made the writing of this book possible through generous financial support.

Thanks to Natalee Caple, for improving my original title, and for her support of this project at many stages. I thank Dennis Cooley for his support and friendship. Mark Hopkins, man about town, lives a double life as a sounding board. Thanks to Kaylen Hann for her careful edits. Thanks to Kirsten Pullen and Sylvia Legris for encouragement, and to the journals *The Capilano Review, filling Station* and *Grain*, where some of these poems were published in earlier versions. Boundless thanks to Coach House Books and its dutiful denizens for their kindness, attention and care.

Thanks to my family and my many friends, with deepest thanks to Mandy Heyens, for supporting me even when I say things like 'I'm going to spend my free time writing plays that would be impossible to produce.'

Thank you for buying this book.

About the Author

Jonathan Ball holds a Ph.D. in English (Calgary) with a focus in creative writing and Canadian literature. He is the author of one previous book of poetry, *Ex Machina* (BookThug, 2009). His writing has appeared in publications across Canada and in the U.S., the U.K. and Australia, including *The Capilano Review, Grain, Prairie Fire, Matrix, The Believer* and *Harper's*. He writes the humour column 'Haiku Horoscopes.' He is the former editor of *dandelion* and the former short films programmer of the Gimli Film Festival. His short film *Spoony B* (Martian Embassy Films, 2005) has appeared on the Comedy Network, and he co-wrote a screenplay that served as the basis for the independent feature film *Snake River* (Ronin Films, 2010). He teaches as a sessional instructor at the University of Manitoba and the University of Winnipeg. Visit Jonathan online at www.jonathanball.com.

Typeset in Oneleigh, designed in 1998 by Toronto's Nick Shinn
Printed and bound at the Coach House on bpNichol Lane, 2010

Edited by Kevin Connolly
Designed by Alana Wilcox
Cover photo, *After the Feast*, by Robert and Shana
    ParkeHarrison, courtesy of the artists

Coach House Books
80 bpNichol Lane
Toronto ON M5S 3J4
Canada

416 979 2217
800 367 6360

mail@chbooks.com
www.chbooks.com